Caring for Betta Fish: An Insider's Guide for Betta Lovers

By Marcus Song

Cover art by Landrum Creations.
http://www.landrumcreations.smugmug.com/

Information Disclaimer:

All information and advice in this book is for entertainment purposes only and should not be considered veterinary advice. If you have health questions for your Bettas, consult a professional veterinarian.

Earnings & Income Disclaimer:

Any earnings statements or income examples are only estimates. There is no assurance you'll do as well. If you rely on the advice in this book, you must accept the risk of not doing well.

Sales results are based on many factors such as the economy, your background, your work ethic, and your business skills and practices. Additionally, there are many unknown risks involved with the Betta breeding business, so it is not suitable for everyone. Therefore the Betta breeding section does not guarantee or imply you'll make any money at all.

You must consult with your accountant, lawyer, and other professional advisors before acting on that or other information in this book. Do your own due diligence when it comes to making business decisions. You agree that our company is not responsible for the success or failure of your business decisions relating to any information presented in this book.

Praise for *Caring for Betta Fish: An Insider's Guide for Betta Lovers*:

"I am so glad you wrote this book! I went to two major book stores in my area. They had betta books, but nothing specific enough to feel comfortable on how to care for the fish. Now I feel confident about helping my fish to live in an appropriate environment. Thanks so much."
Esther Hopper

"Marc, I just wanted to thank you so much for your valuable information which saved me literally hundreds of dollars."
Michael Blair
Miami, FL USA

"I liked that your book is a complete betta owner's manual. As a new owner looking for the basics, you gave me all of the practicalities I needed in order to give my betta the daily care he needs. Yours is a great source of in-depth information and helped me with the questions I had."
Jill Stevens
Atlanta, GA USA

"Your book is great. I'm a newbie with the betta fish and it helped me a lot to make sure it lasts."
Anna Gobshtis
Ontario, Canada

"Your book was fantastic, just finished it. So far it covered everything I can possibly think of. Thank you very much. Looking forward to putting it all into practice."
Jade Crathern

Table of Contents

Introduction

I'd like to congratulate you on getting this guide. You've already done so much for your Betta[1] -- you've rescued him from the prison of the tiny cup the pet store crammed him into, and now you've brought him into your life (or you're about to).

Now with this book you're going to learn how to make him into the happiest, safest, healthiest, most cared-for and indeed the most *spoiled* little fish in the world!

If you've done research online you've probably gotten confused from a lot of conflicting advice. I'm here to set the record straight -- giving you years of not only my own insights and discoveries but those of countless breeders I've had the honor to interview and learn from.

I wrote this book because I understand the pain of losing a Betta even though you thought you did everything right. I've been there too and suffered through that sadness and frustration.

Well, I have good news. Bettas can be very easy to take care of. You've been waiting too long to be able to just relax and enjoy your time with your little one. And this book will let you do just that.

This book is different from most you'll find because I skip the fluff and filler and give straight information. I'm going to give you bullet points, facts, instructions and checklists of useful, specific information you can use immediately.

---

[1] I capitalize "Betta" out of respect for this majestic fish.

I recommend you read this book from cover to cover; by the end you'll know as much about Betta care as any expert out there.

So read on and apply the steps I'll give you. You'll give your little one the best life a pet fish could ever have.

Marcus Song

Chapter 1: History and Habitat of the Betta

Origin of the Betta Name

Although there are many species of Betta, the most common species that is kept and bred is known as the *Betta splendens* or the *Siamese Fighting Fish*. The name "Betta" is said to be derived from an ancient Asian warrior clan known as the *Bettah*, although some accounts differ.

Bettas have their origins in Thailand, Cambodia and Vietnam where, some 150 years ago, the sport of fighting Bettas was actually regulated and taxed by the King of Siam. As popular then as boxing is today, people would bet all of their money, and sometimes their personal belongings and children, on the outcome of just one fight. Thailand was once known as *Siam* which explains the *Siamese Fighting Fish* label.

Although inhumane and no longer practiced widely today, Betta fighting was different from the cockfighting and dog fighting done in the West. While the latter two were contests to see which animal could inflict the most harm on the other, Betta fighting was more a test of bravery to see which fish continued fighting and which gave up first. A Betta was typically fought just once in his lifetime and then bred if he won. (Note -- I'm not defending the practice, just giving you some historical background.)

In the wild, Bettas don't kill each other unless they're in an area that's too small. Normally the loser swims away after the winner flares at him. If there's nipping involved, the loser gets nipped once and then escapes. It's never a fight to the death.

The original Bettas were not fancy and colorful as they are now. Those traits were bred in over the years as Betta made their way from being warrior fish to prized tropical aquarium fish. (Today in fact Bettas are becoming less aggressive as breeders favor their ornamental qualities -- colors and finnage -- to fighting ability.)

Although Bettas are perfectly happy living in small bowls and aquariums, their forefathers made their homes in rice paddies, slow-moving streams, drainage ditches, and large puddles where they foraged for insects and mosquito larvae. So to make them as happy as possible, you should create an aquarium environment as close to natural conditions as you can.

I'll explain more about that in a minute, but first I want to reveal a little bit about Betta biology. Betta fish are known as *anabantids* because they have the ability to breathe atmospheric air thanks to a unique organ called the labyrinth. This accounts for their ability to thrive in low-oxygen water conditions that would kill most other fish. Bettas prefer their water temperature to be in the upper 70° F to lower 80° F range and will become listless in temperatures that fall too far above or below that range. They also prefer shallow water that allows them to easily come up for air.

Your Betta is able to breathe oxygen from the air, and because of that, loves to hang out at the surface.

As the story goes, the King of Siam gave a breeding pair of Bettas to a Dr. Theodore Cantor back in 1840. Several years later the Doctor published a scientific paper about the fish and gave them the Latin name *Macropodus pugnax*. Not long after that it was discovered that a species named *Macropodus pugnax* already existed, and our favorite fish were renamed *Betta splendens*.

Bettas Go International

The first recorded shipment of Bettas outside of Asia took place in 1896 when several breeding pairs were introduced in Germany.

It would not be until 1910 when the first Betta would begin to appear in America thanks to Mr. Frank Locke of San Francisco, CA, who had heard of the species and arranged to import several for his own use. Among the fish that arrived was one that had unusual red fins.

Thinking that he had discovered a different species, he named it *Betta Cambodia* only to later find that he had indeed received the first of the *Betta splendens* that were naturally mutating and developing new color characteristics.

Since that time, breeders have developed many different strains of Bettas resulting in the beautiful and varied colors and finnage that we see today.

Betta Breeds

Spend much time with serious Betta fanciers and you'll hear terms like "veil tail," "delta tail," "crown tail," and "half moon"... and quickly become confused. So I'm going to give you a pain-free introduction to the various lines of the glorious *Betta Splendens*. In a nutshell, the only real difference among the types of Bettas has to do with the tail. I explain as follows...

Veil Tail - Over 80% of fish sold by pet stores are VT males. They're characterized by bottom fin rays being longer than the top rays. (Rays are the "spines" you see in fins.) With fins flared out, VTs look rectangular or diamond-shaped. Most breeders and Betta show enthusiasts look down on the VT as inferior. I think they're mistaken because I think the VT's multiple colors and wavy fins are one of the true miracles of nature.

Round Tail - The tail appears round, hence the name. The circular shape comes from the middle ray of the tail being the longest, and then the rays becoming progressively shorter away from the middle.

Delta Tail - The tail has a triangular shape, which comes from the outermost rays on the tail being the same length as the middle. In Betta shows the widest-tailed of the Delta Tails are the most sought after.

Half Moons - A Delta Tail's tail can become so wide that it forms a half circle (or half moon) shape, at which point it becomes known as the Half Moon Betta. Half Moons are the most popular variety among hardcore Betta fanciers.

Double Tails - These little guys have their tail fork into two halves. DTs are genetic rarities you will never find at a pet store.

Crown Tails - The rays of the tail extend well past the webbing, giving the tail a prickly appearance. Crown Tails are most commonly single rayed. Then breeders bred double rayed Crown Tails which had tail rays branching off. Since then breeders have developed "double double ray" and "double double double ray" Crown Tails, which are the scarcest and costliest Bettas you can buy.

Origin of Betta Colors

The beautiful colors of the Betta that catch our eye were not naturally present when the species was first discovered. Because the Siamese were solely interested in the fighting ability of these fish, breeding practices concentrated on building strength, endurance, and a fierce fighting attitude.

Most of the Bettas from that time were short-finned (to give their opponents less to latch on to), and were a greenish-brown color.

Even in 1840, when the King of Siam made his gift to Cantor, colors still ran towards the drab. By the time the fish began showing up in America, some had begun to develop longer fins and rounded tails, and specks of bright colors could occasionally be found.

There are several basic color genes present or missing in Bettas. Yellow is the base color followed by black, red and blue. There are sub colors as well. For example, the blue gene can be represented by metallic blue, royal blue, or blue-green. The popular royal blue is actually a mixture of the other blues.

These basic color genes, when mixed, are capable of producing fish in the wide variety of colors that we see today. A yellow Betta, for example, has the yellow gene but is missing the black, red, and blue.

It took generations of breeding to produce the vivid colors of today. The gold Bettas resulted from several generations of cross-breeding the Cambodian Black until new generations had no trace of any coloring but gold.

Ever more specialized breeding is required to produce strains such as the Tutweiler Butterfly and the Marbles. The first opaque white Bettas were successfully bred in 1960.

Sometimes certain traits will disappear for generations only to return again when least expected. This is the case with double tail blacks which were once available, disappeared for 20 years, and reemerged in the 1980s.

Table 1 (next page) shows the scientific lineage of the species.

Category: Fish » Freshwater Fish

Kingdom: Animalia

⎯ Phylum: Chordata

⎯ Class: Actinopterygii

⎯ Order: Perciformes

⎯ Family: Belontiidae

⎯ Genus: Betta

⎯ Species: splendens

Table 1

Chapter 2: Betta Fish Characteristics

How Bettas Breathe

Bettas are unique in their ability to breathe the same air that we do. Rather than only use gills, Bettas are equipped with a special organ called a labyrinth which works very much the same way as lungs do in mammals. Because of this, a Betta tank or aquarium does not require aeration, but it is vital the fish be able to reach the top of the water in order to breathe.

The risk to this is that Bettas are also excellent jumpers. This means that the top of the tank should be covered with a mesh screen for maximum safety. You see, even though Bettas can breathe oxygen, their breathing apparatus must be moist to do so. Because of this, it can kill them if it gets dried out (which can happen if your Betta jumps out of his tank).

Do Betta Prefer Confined Areas?

There is evidence to indicate that the male Betta prefers a confined area when breeding, but other than that he appears to be perfectly happy to swim in larger tanks, as long as he has small places in the tank to stake out his territory and hide. So there is no hard and fast requirement to keep your Betta in a small area.

If you notice your Betta swimming in circles a lot, rubbing against the glass, and other sorts of odd behavior that says "Get me outta here!", it indicates he wants to be in a larger tank.

You see, Bettas do like to have room to swim around. They like clean water that's filtered well. The males like to display their toughness to one another - - i.e., to see other Bettas on occasion and flare (puff out their gills and fins) at them. And it's beautiful the way a Betta's fins flow when they're given lots of room to sprint around their tank. Basically the bottom line is this... Bettas have a lot of personality. So as a rule, you should give each Betta enough room to display their individuality.

How to Tell the Male From the Female Betta

As with most animals, male Bettas are more colorful. They also have much longer fins than females. Although some females are known to have brighter colors (and can be just as bright as the males), most are drab and all have short fins.

Of course, make sure that the "females" you bought are not in reality short-finned males, or else you'll be in for a nasty surprise if you put them into a community tank.

> **Betta Lover's Tip:** Here's a quick n' easy test to tell 95% of the time. Put your new Betta in a flat-sided container, and then put the container next to one of your males. If your new Betta flares, you know he's a "he." But if your new Betta displays vertical stripes on the side of her body, she's a female.

Males build bubble nests, although on extremely rare occasions you'll find females that do this too. (By the way, don't be alarmed if a female engages in that sort of behavior. It's perfectly normal for a female to help with bubble nests, and that even includes blowing her own.)

Now here's the way to tell for sure if you little one is a boy or a girl. If your Betta's at least four months old, look for a protruding white spot under her belly. That's an ovipositor or "egg spot," from which females release eggs.

Why Bettas are Known to Have Unusual Behavior Patterns

If you were able to talk to your Betta, they would tell you they have no such thing. Although Bettas may appear to act strangely when compared to other aquarium fish, you must remember that Bettas are not like any other aquarium fish at all.

For example, if you were to observe your Clown Fish lying on his back with a cloud of bubbles gurgling from his mouth, you'd probably be concerned; and rightfully so. If you were observing a male Betta acting similarly, however, you'd be pleased to know that he was simply building a bubble nest.

Bettas frequently stick their heads out of the water not to "look around," but to breathe. They frequently will hover in one place for hours on end. They are very tranquil fish (except when fighting) and find that practice quite enjoyable.

Believe it or not, as your Betta comes to know you, and especially as he comes to know you as his care-giver, he may do a little happy dance or wag his tail as you approach his bowl. And they're not always begging for food -- often they just want your attention. You may notice that when your Betta sees you looking at him, he'll wiggle in the water. He does it because he likes you and wants your attention. And each Betta has their own trademark way of dancing too!

Some Bettas have been known to stick their heads out of the water for a little pat. If you do touch your Betta, be careful not to disturb the slime coat. It's there to protect the fish from infections and disease.

The main thing that's so great about Bettas is how smart, aware of what's going on, and affectionate they are.

Their enthusiasm is what makes Bettas so amazing. I remember back when I got my first one, I couldn't believe how excited he got when he saw me enter the room. (Before I'd thought all fish were dumb and passive.) I quickly bought my second Betta and became hooked for life. It's probably similar for you! Just make sure to give each Betta some quality time with you each day, so that they do not become lonely.

Far from the stereotype of dumb fish, Bettas have strong... and unique... personalities. Some are super mellow, while others will flare at anything they see. They even have unique ways of flaring. I've had Bettas that flare while swimming sideways, some that flare swimming downwards and even one right now who always flares upside down!

I've even had Bettas for whom cleanliness is next to godliness -- particularly with females. They'll go to the bathroom in one specific corner of the tank, underneath part of a plant, in order to keep their home clean.

Other times, you'll have a Betta that even arranges the gravel in their tank. And when you go to move the gravel, they'll arrange it right back the way they want it! Then there's Paul Bunyan (a very big guy) who helps me clean his tank. When I'm using a turkey baster to remove debris, he'll go around pointing out with his nose pieces that I missed.

I could go on and on, but you get the picture. Your Bettas will captivate you with their quirks and sheer intelligence.

Why Bettas Fight

First and foremost, Bettas have a long tradition of fighting to protect their territory from invading males. Remember that in the wild, Bettas lived in relatively small sections of shallow water. There usually wasn't enough food for more than one male, and having an extra male around also threatened the other male's breeding opportunity. For that reason, males would "flex their muscles" to protect their turf. As I said earlier, rarely do Bettas actually fight in the wild, and even more rarely does a Betta get hurt.

Although males mainly hate other males, a male Betta will occasionally attack a female who is either unfamiliar to him or he perceives to be a threat for some reason.

This aggressive trait was magnified and bred into today's fish over the 100 years or more. However, in the past few decades, Bettas have become tamer as aggressiveness is being bred out of them.

How to Prevent Bettas From Fighting

Never put two males together! That's the surest way to prevent them from fighting. If your goal is to introduce a female to the environment, do it slowly. Start by putting the female into a tank and placing it next to the male's tank. Let the male become accustomed to seeing her for a week or so. Then introduce her to the male's environment.

If there are signs of aggression, remove the female and begin the familiarization process again until the male finally accepts the female. Sometimes, for no reason that we understand, a male will reject one female yet accept another. Try switching females if you continue to have a problem.

Some people will take a glass lamp chimney, like the ones that come on a hurricane lamp, and place the wide end down inside the male's bowl. The narrow top should extend beyond the water's surface. Then they place the female inside of the glass chimney and let her stay there for a few days. This serves to let the male become familiar with her and it also gets the female accustomed to the male's water temperature and environment.

As a general rule, it's okay to keep female Bettas together, but you should also be aware of some things. First and foremost, realize that female Bettas establish a hierarchy of most dominant to least dominant. If you put a new female into an established community, keep a lookout for any trouble the first few days she's in the tank. If the new girl is an "alpha female" who'd be likely to bully the others, put her into the tank for a few days using the lamp chimney trick explained above.

Aggressive Posturing

Siamese fighting fish are unique in the way they have such extreme displays to say "back off" to potential opponents. Your Betta flares out his gill covers and fins to make himself look bigger and more menacing. You'll see your little guy doing it mostly when he spots other males. He'll also do it to females sometimes. Another interesting phenomenon noticed by most first-time Betta owners is that your male Betta will even flare up at the sight of his own reflection!

Should you be concerned with your Betta's aggressive display? My experience has been that it's actually a normal and healthy behavior. Just as humans need some stimulation in their lives (as long as it's not too much and stresses them out), so too do Bettas do well that way. I've found that male Bettas kept in complete isolation simply don't have as much of a life expectancy.

So you should induce your Betta to flare himself out aggressively on occasion, in order to maintain his health and vigor? (By the way, if you're going to take your Betta to shows, you'll have to make him flare for the contest judges.) The answer is yes.

Remember that, especially as a beginner, the safest thing is to not put a male Betta in with other Bettas (except for mating). But it's always good for him to see other Bettas and be able to make his occasional display... as long as there is glass separating the male Betta from the other fish.

What Betta breeders do is this. About 30 minutes before feeding, remove the visual barriers you have between the male Bettas. Once they spot each other, that will induce them to have a flaring competition. Then put food in each tank. Once all are done eating, put the visual barriers back.

- If you've got the money for a larger tank set up, there's another option. My personal favorite set up for aggressive males is a 10-gallon tank, with a mesh divider down the middle (to prevent them from harming each other), and a Betta on each side, along with generous amounts of Java moss. That way they can go flare to each other to their hearts' content, then hide behind the moss. From a Betta's perspective, that's a good life!

If you only have one male Betta, then at the very least you should put up a mirror from time to time so that he can flare at his reflection and get some excitement. Don't leave the mirror up for long, however (no more than a few minutes), as that will stress him out.

"Hey! Who's that in the mirror?"

Betta Lover's Tip: If you've just gotten a brand new male fish and he's by himself, don't immediately show him his reflection. He's not used to you or his new home yet. Instead wait till he's comfortable and has become bored.

Sometimes an overly excited male Betta will bite his own tail, resulting in injury. This behavior can be stopped by creating a soothing environment, in order to temper the excitement you now know you should give him from time to time. You can do this by:

1. Having a female Betta in plain view of him (or, if he's tame enough, a female tank mate). For some reason, the little guys don't like to make themselves look like fools in front of the girls.

2. Having him in a tank that does not have any curves. Perhaps because curves cause your Betta to have a distorted reflection, it can cause him to do weird things like chewing on his tail.

3. Putting his aquarium next to your television. The swirl of light from your TV seems to keep your Betta interested. Lava lamps also have this same sort of soothing effect.

4. Putting him in a bigger tank.

5. Making sure his water's clean to maximize healing. Even if your Betta keeps on being crazy and nipping at his own tail, at least the self-inflicted wound won't become infected.

Biting Bettas?

Unlike other aggressive fish like piranhas, Bettas aren't aggressive with people. If you put a finger into your Betta's bowl, he could nip you for the simple reason that he mistakes your finger for food. Or on rare occasions a male might perceive your finger as a threat. Or he could even nip you out of misguided affection, as a way to say "I love you." It all depends on your Betta's personality.

Biting is not a big concern since Bettas are tiny fish and can't inflict much pain on you. Still, there's almost never a good reason for you to put your fingers into the water -- so don't do it, and you'll never get nipped. (If you want to pet your Betta, allow him to surface first -- but make sure you've washed your hands first with organic soap.)

Chapter 3: Buying and Transporting Your Betta

You can find the highest-quality Bettas from professional breeders. If you're interested in doing that, just do a search from any major search engine, or go to AquaBid.com. If the breeder lives near you, consider driving to their location to get your new Bettas. Otherwise, expect to pay $10 to $30 for rush shipping in protective packaging.

I recommend having Bettas shipped to you only when you're sure the weather will always be at least 65 degrees Fahrenheit, day and night, as the Bettas travel via the postal service from the breeder's town to yours. If the temperature could become colder than that, make sure the breeder at least ships the fish with heat packs. Otherwise you might face the sad situation of opening the box and finding your Bettas dead.

Most hobbyists buy Betta fish in a pet store rather than directly from breeders. If you're heading out to pick up a new one, keep these points in mind:

- Look at all the fish in the store, not just the Bettas, to make sure they appear healthy, alert, and well cared for.

- Make sure the tanks are clean and the water appears to be fresh.

- When you look at the Bettas, make sure their colors are bright. (Dull colors could indicate they're stressed.)

- While Bettas may not appear lively in those tiny pet store cups, make sure they at least are alert and not listless.

- Avoid fish with torn fins, bulging eyeballs, loose or misaligned scales, or any kind of abnormal growth or "fur" on their bodies.

- Do not buy a fish if it has just arrived at the store. There is a good chance that it is stressed from being transported and it could also be carrying a disease that has not yet exhibited symptoms.

- Ask the store what their guarantee is. Most good stores offer your money back if your fish dies within a specified period of time or if it comes down with a sickness.

If you see any of the danger signs mentioned above, don't buy a fish. Even if the particular Betta you're interested in looks healthy, there is a chance that he just hasn't started showing the signs of illness like the others have.

While you're checking out the fish, take a look at the general condition of the other pets. If the kittens or puppies appear unhealthy then that's a good indicator that the store personnel do not care for their animals. They don't deserve your business and you don't deserve the problems that poor care will ultimately cause.

Once you have decided you are in a well-managed store, and the Bettas appear to be happy and healthy, it's time to select a fish that appeals to you. The definition of "appeals" can vary widely between people.

Picking the right fish for you can be challenging, since there are so many to choose from. Don't expect your one special fish to wag his tail and look at you with soulful eyes begging to be taken home. They'll probably just ignore you. The solution? Look for the colors and size that appeal to *you*. It really is a personal decision.

Once you select your Betta, carry his cup carefully to the cash register. Try not to jostle him. He's stressed out already and he doesn't need any extra help from you. Stress causes a disease called *ich* and you don't want to start out your new relationship with a sick fish.

Transporting Your New Betta Home

The trip from the pet store to home is fraught with danger for a little fish like your new Betta. Follow these tips to make sure that he arrives alive!

- The main thing to remember when transporting your Betta is that air is more important than water. Make sure that at least three quarters of your Betta's container consists of air.

- Take a small cooler with you.

- Whether your Betta is bagged or in a cup, put a flat layer of newspaper (about 5 or 6 sheets) on the bottom of the cooler to provide a level surface.

- Then place the bag or cup in the center of the cooler.

- Pack wadded newspaper around the cup until all of the open space is filled. This will keep your new companion from being shaken and stirred while you're driving.

- Either place the cooler on the floor or secure it on the front or back seat.

- Avoid bumps and slow down for railroad tracks.

- Don't make sharp turns or sudden stops.

- NEVER leave your Betta in the car while you run other errands. Head straight home! This is particularly true if you live in a very hot or cold climate, or if your Betta is bagged. A bagged Betta will soon run out of air to breathe.

The above rules also work well whenever you need to transport your existing Betta, such as when you're moving to a new house. However, instead of a small cup or bag, you should use a jar that's 8 to 10 inches or so. Fill only the bottom 2 or 3 inches with water. This ensures your fighting fish will have enough air, is at a low enough level that you won't have water splashing out, and leaves enough space so your Betta can't jump out.

Introducing Your Betta to His New Environment

Once you get your new Betta home you are going to have to sensitize him to his new environment. Although we will discuss keeping and raising Bettas more thoroughly in the next chapter, here are some general guidelines to follow...

- Choose a well lit, warm, non-drafty location.

- Do not expose the tank to direct sunlight.

- Never place the bowl next to, on top of, or under a heating or air conditioning vent or radiator.

- Choose a location that has a natural day/night light cycle, such as a room with windows that is dark at night.

- Add some real aquarium gravel. This gives beneficial bacteria a place to colonize and helps to keep the fish's body wastes from floating in the water.

- Add a plastic plant or Java Moss so your Betta has somewhere to hide.

- Float your new Betta, still in the original bag or cup, in the tank for about 15 minutes to give the water temperature time to equalize. Then gently tip the fish into the tank or bowl. Try not to spill any of the water from the cup or bag as it is probably dirty and contaminated with urine and ammonia by now. Discard the cup or bag and the water that was in it.

How to Avoid Having Your Betta Die From "New Tank Syndrome"

An established tank has an ample colony of good bacteria to consume the ammonia and nitrites excreted by your Betta. A new tank -- unless you're able to add some real aquarium gravel as I suggest above -- does not.

Adding the aquarium gravel is important because it's where an aquarium's bacteria are concentrated. Adding it to a new aquarium is known as "seeding," and I'll explain more about it shortly.

But anyway, if you don't have those beneficial bacteria already, you need to take a certain series of steps to avoid having your Betta get poisoned -- an unfortunate phenomenon known as "new tank syndrome."

1. Get a testing kit from your local pet store that measures ammonia and nitrites. Keep testing daily. With a new tank that doesn't have enough good bacteria, you'll notice elevated levels every day.

2. Once a day, replace about 20% of the water with fresh, treated water.

3. If you have Java Moss, put it into the tank. (I explain Java Moss in a little while.)

4. Feed your Bettas as little as possible during this temporary period. Less food for them means they produce less waste.

5. Also avoid using antibiotics on the water. Even though they kill bad bacteria, they also kill the good.

6. After about one to two months, you'll notice that ammonia and nitrite levels are remaining low. Congratulations! That means that you now have a thriving colony of good bacteria and can maintain your Betta's aquarium normally.

Naming Your Betta

To start bonding with your little one, it's best to give him a name! Sometimes it can be daunting to think of one though, since you're pretty much stuck with whatever you choose for the life of your fish.

The best way to fire your imagination, I've found, is to answer this one simple question: What does your Betta look like? From there, you can think of all sorts of things. I named one bright red guy with flowing fins "Fire Monster." As I write this, I'm looking at Queen Elizabeth, a regal, tight-faced old girl who loves to spend her days lounging on top of a leaf.

> **Betta Lover's Tip:** When brainstorming for names, you'll come up with several you like. Write them all down, and then keep the list. That way when you get your next Betta, you'll have a pool of names to draw from!

Chapter 4: Keeping Bettas

Even though Bettas are among the easiest fish to keep, there are certain requirements you need to be aware of so your new friend will have a long and healthy life. Let's start with the basic requirements and move on from there.

Choosing and Setting Up a Tank or Bowl

Tank size is a controversial issue. On a purely physical level, Bettas have an efficient digestive system that doesn't produce much waste, plus they breathe air, so they don't absolutely *need* a larger space. In the wild they basically live in small, stagnant sections of rice patties and other pools of still water and mud holes.

On an emotional level, however, things are different. How happy would you be if you had to spend your whole life in a tiny apartment? Probably the most convincing argument for me though is the fact that Bettas will always use the full tank space you give them.

One Betta I got, Charlie, was sad and lifeless in the little vase he lived in when I got him. He was sickly and lethargic. Then I moved him into a 10-gallon tank and today he's in hog heaven. He spends his days racing and frolicking through his water, exploring pathways through his plants, and flinging around his gravel. He enjoys life and doesn't have to sit crammed into a vase anymore. Vases are for flowers, not Bettas.

So, even though your Betta would be okay living in a gallon-or-so sized jar, there is no reason to consign him to a life of confinement. Bettas will thrive in a goldfish-sized bowl, a small aquarium, or even a larger aquarium under certain conditions.

If you decide to keep your Betta in a small container, remember this:

Although Bettas are used to living in shallow mud holes, rice paddies and swamps, these habitats are part of a natural ecosystem. This means that the water receives nutrients regularly, fresh water constantly flows in and bacteria is flushed out and destroyed by the natural water purification process. And the typical rice paddy is enormous -- about the size of a large pond.

None of this happens in an artificial environment, and the smaller your Betta's habitat is, the more danger they are in due to the quicker formation of adverse environmental conditions.

Overall, your Betta will be happier in a small tank than he will be in a plastic cup or vase. For your little ones to not only survive but to start to be happy, give each Betta a *bare minimum* of 2 gallons of water.

And really I've found (and so have the other breeders I've interviewed) that no Betta -- male or female -- will ever get upset with *too much* room. There's no real upper limit to how big your Betta's tank can be, except for the practical fact that larger tanks are that much more difficult to heat and keep the water clean. So consider the maximum per Betta to be about 10 gallons for each fish.

Besides, there's a possibility (never proved however) that much more than a 10-gallon living space can cause stress since Bettas, being territorial, like to feel cozy.

Some tips for a successful tank set up:

- If you buy a used tank, make sure it's clean and safe. Bacteria are extremely resilient, so take extra measures. Scrub the walls of the aquarium with vinegar or lemon juice. Scrape off any algae. Rinse out the aquarium at least three times with extremely hot water and rinse it using plain hot water. You might be tempted to use soap, but don't; residual soap (which is hard to get rid of entirely) could harm your fish.

- Make sure that a larger tank is wider rather than deeper. That way your Betta won't get tired out swimming to the surface to breathe.

  Betta Lover's Tip: Your Betta's life revolves around the *surface* of the water -- so don't make it hard to get to. Even if there are no females in his tank, your male will still enjoy building a bubble nest at the surface and playing around with it as if training for the day he'll have real babies to raise. This means moving eggs from the bottom up to the nest -- and it's something your male will practice even if he hasn't done any breeding. So the bottom line is that you should aim to have the water depth be no more than 10 inches from substrate (gravel on the bottom) to surface.

- Decide where you are going to place your aquarium. Filled tanks will weigh a lot (each gallon of water is over 8 pounds!), so give some consideration to what you will be placing the tank on.

- Be sure the surface that supports the tank is big enough so the tank is not dangerously close to any edge.

- Do not, under any circumstances, place your tank in an area that will get direct sunlight. Also keep it away from heat and air conditioning sources.

- Choose a large goldfish bowl or small aquarium tank. A water capacity between 5 and 10 gallons per Betta is best. You have your choice of glass or acrylic. Glass is easier to care for and does not need additional support around the edges like acrylic does.

- Depending upon the size of the tank and where it is placed, you may need a water heater to keep the temperature within the Betta's preferred range. (The ideal temperature for a Betta is 78 degrees Fahrenheit. But anything in the 70s is really okay. At 66 to 69, he feels a little uncomfortable and you should consider getting a water heater. When the temperature is 65 or below, definitely get one.)

- When getting a water heater, make sure to read the label to make sure you're getting the proper wattage. A good rule of thumb is to get 5 watts for every gallon. So for a 10 gallon tank, you should get 50 watts. I recommend getting a 100% water-proof, fully submersible heater. Believe me, because you'd be making a long-term investment, it's worth it to pay for high-quality.

- Although Bettas do not *require* it, they won't get mad at you if you install a filter and aeration system. You'll be rewarded with a livelier Betta and you'll benefit from performing less tank maintenance.

- Add a light layer of aquarium gravel. (Use too much and your Betta might get stuck if he buries himself in the gravel.) Don't use marbles, colored stones, or rocks from your back yard, because they can all be contaminated with harmful bacteria. True aquarium gravel will give good bacteria colonies somewhere to form and will naturally filter the fish's bodily waste and leftover food particles.

> **Betta Lover's Tip:** If you're starting a new aquarium for your Betta, and you already have an existing aquarium for your other fish, consider a process known as "seeding." Seeding means using some of the gravel from the existing tank and adding it to your new tank. This has the benefit of transferring existing colonies to your new tank which reduces the time it will take them to grow on their own. That way you avoid a lot of the large spikes in ammonia levels that you often get with new tanks.

- Install real or plastic plants, rock caves, and other decorations that will provide your Betta with plenty of hiding places for when they are feeling insecure or just want to be left alone. Bettas also like to rest on things like horizontal leaves.

- Be careful to choose decorations that are smooth and do not have any rough or sharp edges that can catch and damage your Betta's long fins.

- Also make sure there are no decorations in the tank that your Betta could get stuck in! Bettas love to hide and will sometimes wedge themselves into extremely tight spots that they can't get out of.

- The best plant to have in your Betta aquarium is Java Moss. It's very easy to grow, as it doesn't require direct sunlight, doesn't lay roots, and sinks right to the bottom of the tank. It grows like a weed, but when it grows too big, all you need to do is tear portions of it off and discard them.

  o When you've gotten Java Moss once, you never need to buy it again! To populate a second tank with the moss, all you need to do is tear off a clump of from the first tank. (However, make sure that the Betta in your first tank isn't sick, or else you can sicken the Betta in your second tank.)

  o Basically, the Java Moss will live off of your Betta's waste, which means that not only will the Java Moss decorate your tank and give your Betta a place to hide, it will also keep the water cleaner by reducing harmful nitrite and ammonia levels.

  o If you can't find it at your local aquarium supply store, an excellent place to buy Java Moss (where I get mine) is from a company called Aquarium Garden, which you can find at http://bettalovers.com/aquariumgarden When you go to the site, click the link that says "Aquarium Plant Store." If you're looking for bargains and don't mind the auction process, EBay is another good option, an explanation of which you can find at http://bettalovers.com/ebay

- Avoid fabric plants in your aquarium or any other accessories that contain metal. Metal leeches into the water and poisons your Bettas. (Even trace amounts can have a large effect over time.)

  o However, plastic plants are okay as long as you buy them brand new. Used plastic plants might be full of bacteria and should be avoided. Of course, when you get a plastic plant you don't receive the nitrite-reducing benefits that Java Moss provides.

- Install a lid or mesh screen to keep your Betta from jumping out. They love to jump. If you use a lid, make sure that it has ventilation holes so your fish can come to the surface to breathe. Do not fill the water right up to the bottom of the lid. Leave some "breathing room."

  Betta Lover's Tip: A lid also protects your Betta from predators like your Aunt Martha's visiting cat.

- If your Betta has built a bubble nest, do not, from that point onward, move the tank. The swirling water can destroy your little guy's carefully constructed masterpiece, causing him to feel extremely upset and stressed.

Your Little Buddy's Water

Your Betta needs water that is free of pollutants and chemicals and isn't too far from being pH neutral. You should use properly treated tap water. Here is how the process works...

- First you should call your local water company or look them up online. Ask them if they treat the water with a chemical called "chloramine." If they say yes, you need to get a product from your local pet store called AmQuel, which breaks down chloramines. If they say no, then don't worry about it.

- Water right out of the tap will kill your fish due to chlorine, the chloramine I just mentioned, and other chemicals. Treat the water with a common dechlorinator called Stress Coat (available at any fish store), along with (if you need it) the AmQuel.

- Now you need to age the water. Let the water sit in an uncovered container and air out for a week. That allows time for any dissolved gasses in the water like chlorine to evaporate. Plus it allows pH levels to equalize.

    > **Betta Lover's Tip:** Truth be told, if you're aging the water (and you're sure there aren't chloramines in it), you probably won't need to use any dechlorinators, since any trapped gasses will be released. However, there's always the possibility the water has other chemicals you don't know about. Aging the water will make sure those gasses can also escape.

- Never use purified or distilled water, since the mineral content is too low. Nor should you use one of the carbon water filters that humans use for their drinking water, unless the manufacturer recommends them for aquariums (and normally they don't). There is no need to buy "designer" bottled water either. Your plain, unfiltered tap water should be fine if it is properly treated.

    On the other hand, if you wouldn't drink it straight from the faucet, then the chances are your fish won't like it either. If you do buy bottled water you will still have to treat it, since some brands are treated with chemicals that are bad for your Betta. Get spring water rather than distilled.

    o "Okay," you say, "Good to know this now. But I goofed and have been using bottled water with my Bettas! What should I do now?" The first thing you should do is take a breath and relax. It isn't fatal to your Betta, but it's certainly not as healthy as properly-treated tap water, since it lacks the nourishing minerals that tap water has. Just switch to using properly-treated tap water.

- Change out at least 50% of the tank's water weekly if you are using a filtration system, or 90% if you are not.

    o In general, you don't want to change your Betta's water more often than that. It will stress him out. And with Bettas, an excessive amount of stress can be fatal.

- Make sure the new water is nearly the same temperature as the water remaining in the tank. Dramatic temperature changes can harm your Betta.

- Buy and use a water testing kit available from any fish store. You should measure ammonia and nitrites, keeping them as close to 0 as possible (especially the ammonia). The pH levels should ideally be 6.8 to 7.0 -- slightly acidic to neutral.

> **Betta Lover's Tip:** Don't worry about it if the water's pH isn't in that exact range. Bettas can adjust. The main thing is to not make drastic changes to the pH level. For your little ones, a *stable* pH is the most important thing. Additionally, the chemicals used to adjust pH have been observed to cause Bettas to become sick and even die.

- If you're not using a filtration system, it is important you change the water at least once per week. Follow this procedure:

  - Remove the plant and rinse it under de-chlorinated water.

  - Stir up the gravel to cause the waste particles to float freely.

  - Pour out approximately 90% of the water.

  - Wipe away any algae or other material from the sides of the tank.

    > **Betta Lover's Tip**: Don't do an extremely thorough job wiping the tank. A normal aquarium builds up colonies of good bacteria, which you want to keep!

  - Add enough aged water to bring the tank back to its normal level.

  - Start the process of preparing and aging the water for next week's change.

Tank cleaning tips

Cleaning your tank isn't difficult, but it is important. A large percentage of ailments Bettas face really boils down to poor water quality. Your Betta will definitely wag his tail more if you keep his environment clean.

So make it a point to schedule maintenance and cleaning time every week. Follow these tips for guaranteed success:

- Use a siphon to clean out the accumulated deposits from the gravel, especially if you have an under-gravel filtration system.

- Use an algae scraper to clean the glass and ornaments

  Betta Lover's Tip 1: Algae live off the dissolved poop of your Betta. So if you spot algae in your Betta's aquarium, it's an indicator you haven't been keeping his water clean enough. Don't sweat the algae itself, however. It's the excess poop that's bad for your Betta, not the algae!

  Betta Lover's Tip 2: Under all circumstances avoid algae-killing products containing chemicals. Bettas are too fragile.

  Betta Lover's Tip 3: The best way to get rid of algae is to change the water often enough and avoid putting the tank where it gets direct sunlight (since algae -- like any other plants -- are photogenic). There -- I've just saved you from having to spend $19.95 plus shipping on an anti-algae product!

- Clean the filters according to the manufacturer's instructions. If you have to replace filter media, try to leave some of the existing media in place so you do not remove all of the beneficial bacteria colonies that have formed.

- Use a clean utensil to scoop out the water until you have removed between 50% and 90% (depending upon whether you are using a filtration system or not).

- Add new water which has been aged and treated for chlorine and to which you have added any health additives. Make sure that the water is near the same temperature as the remaining water in the tank. The easiest way to add water in a larger tank is to use a clean bucket which has never held any detergents or chemicals. Run a siphon hose from the bucket to the tank to avoid creating splashes and disturbing the gravel, ornaments, or fish.

- Remember to leave breathing room between the top of the tank and the cover.

If you notice a foul smell from your Betta's bowl, it usually means that the water is not clean enough (which often happens with smaller tanks). The most common cause of a bad smell is excessive ammonia. That means you're not cleaning the tank thoroughly enough. In cases such as that, remove your Betta from the tank and give everything in it a thorough rinsing with hot water.

Tips for choosing a filtration system

- Match the filter to the size of the tank. Your pet shop salesperson can help you make the right choice.

- Decide between an activated charcoal or an under-gravel filter. Both work equally well in a 10 gallon tank. The under-gravel may be a better choice for larger tanks. The under-gravel filter uses a flat plastic tray that gets placed below the gravel layer in the tank. Water is drawn down through the gravel and into the filtering holes in the tray. Once in the tray, the water passes through a system of tubes which are lined with bacteria cultures that break down the waste and pollutants. The only drawback is you have to either remove the gravel when it's time to clean the filter, or purchase a special filter siphon to suck up the debris that accumulates in the gravel.

  Small tanks can also use a box filter which attaches to a corner or inside wall of the tank. The water gets drawn into the filter, passed through a fiber filter and a layer of activated charcoal, and then gets discharged back into the tank. Caution: Smaller fish can get sucked up into the filtration chamber. While that probably won't kill them, it does cause them stress.

- Larger tanks can use an outside power filter. These are attached to the outside of the tank wall. They use a pump to draw the water into a box containing special filtering material and activated charcoal. These filters are especially designed for larger tanks with a large fish population. They are probably overkill for your Betta's habitat. Plus keep in mind that Bettas, who live in stagnant water in the wild, like their tank to be as quiet as possible.

- Use strong caution when it comes to using filters that are powered, as they can stress out your Betta. Instead you should keep the water as still and silent as possible. So another option to consider is getting a sponge filter. Not only are they the quietest but they're also the cheapest of filters. The brand I use and recommend is the Hydor Bioflo. If you can't find them at your local pet store, you can get them online here: http://bettalovers.com/filter1

- If your chosen filter doesn't provide an air pump, you may choose to purchase one separately. If you change and maintain the water regularly, and you give your Betta "breathing room" at the top of the tank, a pump is not a necessity. If you do decide to purchase one, you will need to match the pump to the water capacity of the tank. Ask your pet supply salesperson for help.

Putting Your Betta With Other Fish

One of the saddest myths about Bettas is that they're solitary fish. When a Betta is all alone in the world, he becomes lethargic and depressed and sulks around. The fact is Bettas need the stimulation that exposure to other Bettas or Betta-friendly fish brings them. You never need to force your Betta to be lonely as long as you follow these guidelines:

- Until you know better, never put two males into the same tank. And until you've learned their personalities never put a male and a female into the same tank either, unless you are breeding. We'll discuss breeding in a later chapter.

- Once you've learned enough about the personalities of your males, you can put some of them in with others. It's actually rare to find a male so aggressive he must always be kept by himself.

- When you first put multiple Bettas in a tank together, expect to see posturing and maybe even a couple of nips. Males and females alike can do this. As long as the behavior stays low level and only lasts a little while, it's normal. Your Bettas are figuring out their pecking order. However, if you see fins starting to be shredded, it's not normal, and you need to separate the Bettas.

"Who you lookin' at?"

Betta Lover's Tip: Once you've learned their personalities, you may be able to get away with having up to two males and 2 or so females together in a 10+ gallon tank -- provided your tank is full of plants like Java Moss. This comes close to simulating conditions in nature. Basically, each male will have his own little "house" at an opposite end of the aquarium from the other one. He'll build a bubble nest, living a normal life and mating with a female on occasion. (Be sure to get the female out of there once the eggs are laid, however.)

- Don't put your Betta into the same tank with Gouramis. They are distant cousins and they may fight. Also avoid the Platy and Variatus.

- Avoid putting Bettas into a tank with any species of fish that is long-finned.

- While it might be unlikely that your Betta will fight with other species, there is a chance that other species like guppies will try to nibble on their long and tasty-looking fins, so keep an eye out. In fact most of the time, I've discovered, it is the Betta who is the victim of aggression.

- Some good companion fish to Bettas are Cory varieties, Barb varieties, swordtails, angelfish, and the various types of catfish. And as a general rule, Bettas do well with fish that are too big to be harmed, plus those that live in similar conditions in the wild (i.e., warm, fresh water). So for example that means don't put goldfish in with your Bettas, since they're a cold water fish. A lot also depends on the individual personalities of the other fish.

- Snails are popular among hobbyists because they keep the tank clean by consuming organic matter and uneaten food. They're like living water filters. So consider getting a snail for your little one's tank.

    Betta Lover's Tip: If you notice a snail population explosion after putting a snail in the tank, it means there's too much uneaten food in the tank, and you're either overfeeding your Betta or aren't cleaning the water enough. By the way, in case you're wondering, snails are unisex (posses both male and female genitalia), so one snail is all it takes to reproduce.

- If you do introduce a Betta to an existing community, don't do it at a time when you won't be around for at least a few hours to see what develops. Remove the Betta at the first sign of conflict.

    Betta Lover's Tip: A lot of the time a male will flare at first but will soon calm down when they discover the other fish won't attack them.

- When it comes to having your Betta live with other fish, basically what it all boils down is your Betta's individual personality. Every Betta is unique. Some are nice, others are bullies.

- It also boils down to how *active* the other fish are. If your Betta's bubble nest gets destroyed by another fish swimming around too fast, it will cause your Betta an extreme amount of stress.

- A lot of times aggression issues are caused by Bettas not being able to stake out enough territory for themselves, so they're simply scaring off the invader. Remember, two and a half gallons are the bare minimum a Betta needs to be content (and some Bettas require more), so if you've got a 10-gallon tank, keep no more than 4 Bettas in it. Have plants and decorations in the tank to serve as territorial barriers.

- If you've got an overly aggressive male who must stay by himself, at least allow him to see and flare against other males as I have talked about.

- Remember that Bettas need a water temperature in the 80° F range, so don't introduce your Betta to a tank with water that's out of that range.

- I shouldn't have to say this… Bettas are freshwater fish, so saltwater aquariums are off limits!

Chapter 5: Betta Feeding

Bettas are carnivores. That means they eat meat. Feeding your Betta a vegetarian diet will make him sick because he will not get the protein he needs. If your dietary beliefs do not allow you to feed meat products to your Betta, don't buy one!

- Bettas have small appetites, so it's important not to overfeed them. Never feed more than your fish can consume in 2-3 minutes.

   > **Betta Lover's Tip:** Is your Betta not eating? Take a look at the temperature of his water. Bettas are happiest at 78° F and become finicky when the water drops too much below that.

- You can purchase fresh or frozen Betta food from your pet supply store. The healthiest product (plus the one most used by breeders) is called Hikari Bio-Gold. If you can't find that at your local store, a simple web search will turn up multiple vendors.

- The dispenser you're supposed to use with the Hikari Bio-Gold is difficult to work with, so I recommend putting the food into a sealable plastic food storage bag and simply discarding the package.

- How to feed your little guy:

   1. Soak the dry Bio-Gold pellets in water for 3 minutes to let them swell.

   2. Pick up the pellets with an eye dropper.

   3. Drop them in.

- Bettas can be finicky, so don't be alarmed if your fish doesn't eat the food on a particular day -- especially when you first get them. It might take up to a week before your Betta gives in and eats. Don't worry, he won't starve in that time period. Just remove any food particles uneaten after 3 minutes, and then try again the next day.

- o Before you get concerned -- removing food particles is easy. Just use a turkey baster.

Little Bites For Bettas: Giving the Best Treats

- If you want to give your Betta an occasional "treat" feed some frozen Mysis shrimp. They have a higher protein and fat content than the traditional Brine shrimp do.

- Blood worms (despite what many pet stores tell you) are okay *only* as a very occasional treat. It's very easy for a Betta to eat too much and get swim-bladder condition. So at best a blood worm should just be a treat for when your Betta has been especially good.

  Betta Lover's Tip: If you do give the infrequent bloodworm to your little guy, make sure not to breathe the dust from the package! Jesse, a reader from Newport, RI, wrote, "I had suffered severe sneezing fits, runny nose, itchy watery eyes and neck/chin areas that lasted for days at a time. Who would suspect a fish food could cause such severe allergies?"

- Your Betta may also eat the occasional fly or mosquito unlucky enough to fall into the tank.

- I once read about a Betta who would eat roaches that crawled into the tank. Personally, I would rather not live somewhere that I had to worry about my Betta eating roaches.

- Other good treats are a tiny piece of white meat chicken, a tiny piece of steak, and a tiny cooked and cooled-down pea with the skin peeled off.

  Betta Lover's Tip: Live food can carry parasites, so consider them like "candy" for your Bettas -- i.e., just for special occasions.

- If there is food left over then you are overfeeding and contributing to both his poor health and the poor health of the aquarium environment. Decaying food upsets the delicate ecosystem balance. It is the #1 cause of bacterial growth, which can harm (and even kill) your Betta.

- There is some disagreement about this issue, but I have found through my extensive research and experience that most Bettas only need to be fed once per day. This most closely approximates a Betta's feeding experience in nature. If you want to feed twice per day, remember you are running the risk of overfeeding plus you will likely end up having to clean the aquarium more frequently to counteract the additional waste buildup.

- Use your fingers to drop the food particles one by one on the water's surface. The Betta will come up to feed. Bettas are not bottom feeders. Their upturned mouth is evidence of the fact that they are naturally suited to catch their food as it falls from the sky. Sit there with your fish throughout the 2-3 minute eating process, feeding him as he swallows each pellet. Feeding time is a great chance for you and your Betta to bond, so use it! Don't just sprinkle the food in and leave.

- Don't be surprised if your Betta grabs a morsel of food and then dashes off to some safe cover to eat it. Fish often feel threatened when they are eating even if there are no other fish in the tank.

  > **Betta Lover's Tip:** According to a biologist who contributed to this book, the best time to feed a Betta is about an hour after sunrise or an hour before sunset. This coincides with the time that insects naturally swarm and land in the water in the fish's natural environment. If those times aren't convenient, then pick some that are. Your fish will adjust.

- Regardless of the time that you choose, try to feed your Betta at the same time every day. This gets them into a routine. After a while you will swear they're wearing a wristwatch because they'll start wagging their tail and coming to the surface at the appointed feeding time.

How to Go on Vacation Without Starving Your Betta

A big advantage of Bettas compared with other pets like dogs is that it's easy to take vacations when you're a Betta parent. The following insider secrets will keep your Bettas as healthy as possible while you're gone...

- If you're going to be gone for less than 10 days or so, consider simply having your Betta fast during that time. Bettas have highly efficient metabolisms and can go for literally months without eating if they have to (not that I advocate that of course).

Betta Lover's Tip: It won't be as bad if you feed just before leaving and then immediately upon returning.

- Do not get your Betta one of those slow-release blocks of food that are supposed to feed your fish for 7 to 14 days. They can play havoc on your little one's water -- and the danger from that is far worse than if they simply fasted.

- If you're going to be gone for longer than 10 days, have a trusted friend, family member, neighbor or pet sitter check in and change the water, feed your Betta, make sure the temperature is okay, and so on -- give them a thorough checklist of things they should do, based on what you're learning in this book.

Chapter 6: Health Concerns and Treatments

Like any fish, your Betta is subject to health risks. You can reduce these risks by...

- Not handling the fish, which can injure its slime coat

- Using proper health additives.

- Maintaining a clean tank.

- Feeding your fish the proper diet in the proper quantities.

If you do need to lift your Betta out of his cage, do not use your hands if you can avoid it. Instead use a net. In the extremely rare case you ever would need to use your fingers, lift him with the palm of your hand rather than squeezing him between your fingers.

> **Betta Lover's Tip:** Before handling your Bettas, wash your hands! As reader Vicky Gonzales wrote me, "I saw a guy in our local pet store stick his entire dirty arm into a tank to retrieve a bunch of dead bettas, and he was wondering why they were dying?" To avoid possible chemical poisoning, make sure to use hand soap that's organic and non-toxic.

I have assembled a Troubleshooting Guide showing you the most common symptoms of trouble you may notice on your Betta. This chart is not a substitute for medical advice, which you should always seek if you have any doubt about the health of your fish.

Some pet stores maintain fish professionals on site. You can also check with a vet who works with fish, or you might want to visit some of the Betta resources on the Internet. I have listed several of them at the end of this book. You can search the Internet for more.

Troubleshooting Guide

While it may look like there is no chance of ever raising a healthy Betta fish, remember that most of these conditions below can be avoided with proper diet and nutrition, using the proper health additives in the water, and maintaining a safe and clean tank environment.

If your fish has symptoms not presented below, seek medical advice from a vet or trained fish breeder.

Problem 1:

Fish die suddenly or stay near the water surface or bottom for extended periods of time.

Fish may lose their appetite and become sluggish.

Lose a lot of their color.

Analysis and Treatment:

1) Possible poisoning.

- Check water for presence of chlorine or other chemicals.

- Examine fish for signs of parasites or bacterial infection.

- If anything is found, change out 100% of the water with treated, aged water. Check the storage container that you age your water in for presence of chemicals as well.

2) Possible low dissolved oxygen levels.

Even though Bettas can breathe air, excessively low oxygen levels can affect health especially if there is not enough breathing room at the top of the tank.

- Check oxygen levels first thing in the morning when levels are the lowest.

- Consider installing an air pump if excessive low levels consistently appear.

3) Possible Peracute Bacterial disease. Proper diagnosis requires post mortem lab examination.

Problem 2:

Fish are rubbing against ornaments and may give off a silver "flash" when their underbody is exposed.

Analysis and Treatment:

This is indicative of skin irritation.

- Check water ammonia, nitrite and pH levels. Ammonia and nitrites should be 0; pH should be between 6.8 and 7.0. Adjust as necessary.

- Examine the fish for evidence of ectoparasites including flukes, *Trichodina*, or white-spot.

Problem 3:

Fish appear to have a hard time breathing or appear to be gasping for air.

Analysis and Treatment:

- Check for low dissolved oxygen levels first thing in the morning when the levels are at their lowest.

- Check water ammonia, nitrite and pH levels. Ammonia and nitrites should be 0; pH should be between 6.8 and 7.0. Adjust as necessary.

- Check that all filter materials are clean and that the filter is operating correctly.

Problem 4:

Fish refuses food and there is the presence of cloudy grey areas on the skin.

Analysis and Treatment:

- Examine fish for parasites. Do a water change and treat with aquarium salt (half a teaspoon per gallon of water).

- Check water ammonia, nitrite and pH levels. Ammonia and nitrites should be 0; pH should be between 6.8 and 7.0. Adjust as necessary.

- Possible bacterial infection. Treat water with Methylene Blue (described in Problem 14).

Problem 5:

Fish appear nervous or shy.

Possible presence of split or shredded fins.

(If fins appear to be wasting away, it's possible fin rot. See Problem 24.)

Analysis and Treatment:

- Check water ammonia, nitrite and pH levels. Ammonia and nitrites should be 0; pH should be between 6.8 and 7.0. Adjust as necessary.

- Excessive organic pollution. Clean tank and check filter.

- Possible bacterial disease. Treat fish for bacterial infection as described in Problem 14. Check fish for lesions, swelling and ulceration.

Problem 6:

Presence of excessive skin mucus.

Presence of grayish slime or mucus trailing from the body.

The fish may also exhibit rubbing or flashing characteristics or have trouble breathing.

Analysis and Treatment:

- Check water ammonia, nitrite and pH levels. Ammonia and nitrites should be 0; pH should be between 6.8 and 7.0. Adjust as necessary.

- Possible presence of ectoparasites.

- Do a water change and treat tank with aquarium salt.

Problem 7:

Loss of color.

Development of horizontal stripes.

Analysis and Treatment:

- These are signs that a Betta feels stressed. Whatever has changed in your fish's life recently (for example, when you're changing his water or even when you've just put a new decoration in his tank) is often the condition that is causing your fish to feel stress.

- Always avoid doing things that cause your Betta to turn pale. If it happens from a water change, make sure that the new water is the same temperature as the old. Also make sure that it has the same minerals, chemicals, and pH level. Also avoid being rough with your Betta.

Problem 8:

Evidence of skin lesions, ulcers, swelling or inflammation, open wounds or lesions that fail to heal within 2-3 days.

Analysis and Treatment:

- Injury caused by sharp object in the tank such as damaged or improper ornaments. Remove object.

- Ectoparasite infection. Treat tank with aquarium salt.

- Bacterial infection. Apply Methylene Blue to tank. If that does not work, use Aquarium Tetracycline.

- Check water ammonia, nitrite and pH levels. Adjust as necessary.

- Excessive organic pollution. Clean tank and check filter.

Problem 9:

Bright red or white lesions.

Analysis and Treatment:

- Check skin for lice, leeches or anchor worms.

- Change water and treat tank with aquarium salt (half a teaspoon per gallon of water)

Problem 10:

Swollen body, Betta floating on his side at the top of the water unable to balance himself, maybe even has trouble breathing.

Analysis and Treatment:

- Your Betta is constipated.

- Instead of his regular food, give him a small piece of a cooked (and cooled-down) pea with the outer skin removed. The fiber will act as a natural laxative.

  o Note: Your Betta may be finicky and go on a hunger strike for up to a week before he eats the pea.

- Twice a day for 20 minutes put your Betta into a small tank that has 1 tablespoon of Epsom Salt (available at drugstores) dissolved in each gallon of water.

    Betta Lover's Tip: The #1 cause of constipation in Bettas is feeding them too much.

Problem 11:

Swollen abdomen which may be combined with raised scales, reddening on the fins, abdomen, body or fins, exophthalmos (bulging eyes)

Analysis and Treatment:

Viral infection. Quarantine from other Bettas in a clean tank.

- Systemic bacterial infection. Apply Methylene Blue. If that does not work, use Aquarium Tetracycline.

- Heart or kidney disease (fatal).

- Internal parasites. Use Hex-A-Mit or Metrozol, as described in Problem 20, below.

- Genetic disorder. Do not breed.

- Intestinal blockage (fatal).

Problem 12:

Gasping for air or difficulty breathing even though dissolved oxygen levels are within tolerances.

Analysis and Treatment:

- Possible viral infection.

- Remove infected fish to his own tank, quarantined from the other Bettas, and giving him the best possible food and water. Unfortunately, viruses are hard to treat and the best thing you can do is facilitate the fish's natural healing.

Problem 13:

Small white spots on skin and fins resembling salt crystals. May be accompanied by thickened mucus.

Betta scrapes himself against aquarium decorations as if to scratch an itch.

Eventually, fish may lose energy and lie listlessly at bottom of tank.

Analysis and Treatment:

- Bacterial infection known as Ichthyophthirius (white spot). Also known as "ich" or "ick." Check skin scraping.

- Add one teaspoon of pure rock salt (available at any grocery store) to your Betta's tank for each gallon of water. This is a much cheaper option than buying medication and usually just as effective.

- Increase the temperature of the water to 81-83 degrees during treatment. This speeds up the life cycle of the bacteria so they die and fall off the Betta.

- In case the rock salt does not work (although usually it does), treat the infected fish with ich medication, which is readily available anywhere aquarium supplies are sold.

Problem 14:

White or unusually-colored patches resembling cotton. May be accompanied by inflammation or patches of eroded skin.

Analysis and Treatment:

- Saprolegnia (fungus) infection.

- Columnaris infection (mouth fungus/cotton wool disease).

- Treat tank with Methylene Blue, an anti-fungal medication available at your local pet store.

What Is Methylene Blue?
An anti-fungal treatment that's a good all-purpose cure for your Bettas, as it also sterilizes the water against many forms of bacteria. Whenever your Betta is feeling under the weather, it never hurts (and often helps) to apply Methylene Blue. Some breeders use Methylene Blue every time they change their Betta's water. Simply add 12 drops of Methylene Blue to each gallon of water (or follow whatever the directions on the package say).

- If Methylene Blue does not work, use aquarium tetracycline, a strong antibiotic available at your local pet store or through multiple sources online.

Problem 15:

Skin swelling.

Analysis and Treatment:

- Parasitic cysts. Change water and treat tank with aquarium salt.

- Damage caused by other fish or ornaments.

- Bacterial infection but only if accompanied by inflammation and raised scales.

- Treat tank with Methylene Blue.

- Internal tumors. Unfortunately Bettas have been increasingly getting cancer due to genetic reasons. If you have a Betta die from cancer, do not get any more fish from that bloodline, and do not breed any from that blood line.

Problem 16:

Unusual growths or protrusions on the skin or fins.

Analysis and Treatment:

- Tumors.

- Carp pox. Looks like melted wax has been poured over the fins or skin.

- Papillomas (warts). May appear as large, smooth or cauliflower-like growths. May be white, red or pink.

- Llymphocystis.

There are no available remedies for any of these conditions. Most will disappear on their own over time.

Problem 17:

Corneal Opacity (cloudy eyes).

Analysis and Treatment:

- Damage caused by other fish or ornaments.

- Poor nutrition. Check diet.

- Check water ammonia, nitrite and PH levels. Adjust as necessary.

- Bacterial infection. Apply anti-bacterial treatment.

- If eye has white coating, then it's a possible fungus infection. Apply either Methylene Blue or a product called Eye Fungex. (Both are available at your local pet store or through the Internet.)

Problem 18:

Spinal deformities.

Analysis and Treatment:

- Electrical shock. Check all electrical connections in tank.

- Improper use of organophosphates for medical treatment.

- Poor nutrition. Check diet.

- Genetic conditions.

- Presence of toxins. Use a water testing kit.

Problem 19:

Fish unable to retain balance, may have difficulty swimming in proper orientation, fish turn over on back when not swimming.

Analysis and Treatment:

- Swim-bladder condition caused by viral or bacterial infection or other organ disease. Quarantine from other Bettas and apply Methylene Blue.

- Kidney disease or intestinal blockage (fatal).

- Most likely cause: swim bladder condition from overfeeding. Your little guy will eat foods, particularly treats like brine shrimp and bloodworms, to excess. The solution therefore is to cut down on the amount you feed your Betta.

Problem 20:

Bettas die for no apparent reason.

Presence of worms hanging from the anus.

Excessive or rapid weight loss.

Lethargy.

Analysis and Treatment:

- Endoparasites.

- There are two good products that work on internal parasites. One is called Hex-A-Mit. The other is Metrozol. Your local pet store should carry one or the other. If not, check online.

- When Bettas get parasites, usually the source can be traced to them eating live food, particularly live brown worms.

Problem 21:

One or both of your Betta's eyes are bulging. Betta may also lose his appetite and become less energetic.

Analysis and Treatment:

- This is a bacterial infection known as Pop Eye.

- Treat with an antibiotic called Ampicilex.

- During treatment, change Betta's water twice as often as you normally do.

- To prevent problem from reoccurring, make sure to keep to your regular water cleaning schedule. (The usual cause of Pop Eye is not keeping your Betta's water clean.)

Problem 22:

Betta's scales develop an extremely raised, prickly appearance resembling pine cones. Abdomen swells. Fish dies within days.

Analysis and Treatment:

- Your Betta has dropsy, a fatal disease with unfortunately no cure.

- Immediately quarantine infected fish and isolate from the other Bettas.

- Apply 1 teaspoon of salt per gallon of water. Also apply Aquarium Tetracycline. If the dropsy is caught early enough, there's a slight possibility the fish could recover.

Problem 23:

Betta covered with a thin rust- or gold-colored film. Fish may lose its color, scrape against items in the aquarium, and lose its appetite.

Analysis and Treatment:

- Your Betta has a parasite known as Velvet.

- Quarantine infected fish. (Velvet is infectious.)

- Follow same procedure as you would with ich (Problem 13).

Problem 24:

Your Betta's fins are withering away and disintegrating.

Analysis and Treatment:

- This is a condition known as Fin Rot.

- Apply a product called "Neosulfex" by Aquatronics (available at almost all pet stores that sell aquarium supplies). It should take about a month to work, so be patient.

- If Neosulfex is not fully effective, combine it with a product called Jungle Fungus Eliminator.

- Make sure to keep to regular water cleaning schedule. (The most common cause of fin rot is dirty water.)

Problem 25:

Your Betta stays at the very bottom of the tank (maybe even burying himself in the gravel), only surfacing to get air.

Analysis and Treatment:

- There is a problem with your little guy's water.

- See Chapter 4 for instructions on keeping the water at the right pH and temperature and free from chlorine.

Emergency First Aid

Although you can't perform mouth-to-mouth on an injured fish, there are some simple first aid techniques you should be aware of.

- Remove any fish that are exhibiting signs of illness from the general fish population.

- Test the water for ammonia, nitrites, pH, and oxygen levels. The ammonia and nitrites should be 0; pH should be between 6.8 and 7.0. Dissolved oxygen levels should be above 60%.

  Betta Lover's Tip: An easy way to reduce nitrites and ammonia in your water is to put in a piece of Java Moss.

- Remove any dead fish at once. Refrigerate in a baggie until you can get it to a vet or lab for examination.

- Perform a 50% water change using aged and treated water.

- Remove live plants and conduct a salt treatment (see below).

How and When to Perform a Salt Treatment

Although your Bettas are freshwater fish, they can benefit from a bit of salt now and then. Salt helps to heal certain skin injuries, assists in promoting the formation of the slime coat, combats some parasites, and helps with nitrate uptake.

Salt will kill live plants so remove them during the treatment and for about one week after.

Type of Salt to Use

Ordinary table salt is fine as long as it does not have any additives such as iodine. Rock or Kosher salt is preferred.

Using Salt for Well Fish

Salt is effective preventative against nitrate poising, certain parasites, and it promotes good slime coat development.

Add one half ounce of salt per gallon of water to a new tank, and about one-quarter ounce per gallon when doing less than a full water change.

Using Salt for Sick Fish

Use a dip for treating parasites. Dipping means immersing the fish in a salt and water solution for up to 30 minutes or so. Use a mixture of 3% salt to 97% water.

Use a bath to treat the entire tank for stress, nitrite poisoning, and some parasites. Create a 1% salt to a 99% water solution. Continue the bath for 1-3 weeks.

How to Perform a Dip

- Place 4 teaspoons of salt in a clean bucket that has never held detergents or chemicals.

- Slowly add one gallon of water from the aquarium. Swirl the water as you pour to dissolve the salt. Stir to complete the dissolution using a clean wooden spoon.

- Slowly and gently place the fish into the bucket for up to 30 minutes.

- Watch the Betta closely. If he exhibits any signs of discomfort or stress from the salt, remove him from the bucket and return him to the tank immediately.

How to Perform a Bath

For Stress:

- Add 1 teaspoon of salt per gallon of tank water by adding some tank water to a clean container that has never held detergents or chemicals.

- Stir the solution with a wooden spoon until the salt is completely dissolved.

- Slowly pour the solution into the tank.

- Using a small container, dissolve the salt in a small quantity of water taken from the tank. Once it is completely dissolved, slowly add the solution to the tank.

- Change 25% of the water weekly but do not add more salt.

Boosting Your Betta's Life Expectancy

The typical Betta lives about two to five years (and on rare occasions as long as seven), depending on many factors. Some you can control and some you can't. Generally the better you take care of them, the longer they'll live. Use the following guidelines to know whether your little one is likely to be with you for a long, long time.

1. **Genetics.** Unfortunately of course there's nothing you can do about this. Bettas with traits more closely resembling their wild ancestors (shorter, rounder fins; plainer colors; etc.) tend to live longer. Those with exotic features got that way due to highly selective breeding... which unfortunately has the drawback of requiring a certain amount of inbreeding.

2. **Living Conditions.** Fortunately this is an area you can do something about. The number one rule is to keep your Betta's water as clean as possible. (Follow the directions in chapter 4.) Most diseases are caused by dirty water. Next, make sure to feed your Betta the most nutritious food possible. (See chapter 5.) Then work on the quality of life tips you've learned like giving your Betta the socialization he needs and avoid too much stress.

3. **The Right Amount of Stress.** Bettas can easily become too stressed out, which dramatically lowers their life expectancy.

    o A huge source of stress for both male and female Bettas is the breeding process. Sadly, if you want to breed a particular fish, expect that his lifespan will be cut short.

    o Keep your Betta's life calm. See Problem 7 of the Troubleshooting Guide in this book.

    o To give your Bettas the right amount of stimulation, you need to allow them a healthy amount of social interaction. See what I said earlier on how to allow your male Betta to aggressively display. Females can be kept together... but you should follow the instructions I have given you for that.

Chapter 7: Better Betta Breeding Basics

This is a quick guide that will end your confusion about breeding your little ones.

The Nuts and Bolts of Breeding

Breeding Bettas can be fun but it can be a challenge as well. Just because you are interested in breeding Bettas, it doesn't mean that the Bettas will be. Your job is to set the mood for love.

Also keep in mind that you might become *too* successful. The typical highly-fertile female can produce a few hundred eggs... meaning you might wind up with a few hundred Bettas! The good news though is that your local pet store will often be happy to take them off your hands -- and often for as much as a dollar a piece.

When the time comes that you're ready to give it a shot, follow these tips and you could be rewarded with a brood of new fry.

Preparing the Breeding Tank

Set up a 10-gallon tank especially for breeding. Place a few live or plastic plants in the tank so the female has somewhere to hide, but do not add gravel or other ornaments. Follow the same water handling procedures as you would for a regular Betta tank.

Install a box filter that uses a fiber filter material, not charcoal. Run the filter for a week or so, before introducing the fish, to give the bacteria culture time to grow. If you want, you can remove some filter material from your main tank and use it to seed or jumpstart the bacterial growth.

Selecting a Breeding Pair

Chances are your existing Betta will be too old to breed. Your breeding pair should be between 8 months and 12 months old. The average pet store Betta is over a year old when it is sold. Plus pet store Bettas are, sadly, typically too stressed to be good breeding candidates.

Because of that, it's advisable to purchase your breeding pairs from a reputable Betta breeder. I say "pairs" because it's a good idea to buy more than one pair in case there are compatibility issues or the fish just refuse to breed.

Choose ones that have the color traits that you are seeking. Never breed an overly aggressive male, because aggression is a trait that gets passed down.

Starting two weeks beforehand, feed both Bettas live Mysis or brine shrimp, bloodworms and other protein-rich meat in order to trigger their mating hormones.

Introducing the Male

Introduce the male to the tank first.

Place the female in a separate 5-gallon (or so) tank and place it in sight of the male. This should trigger the male to begin building a bubble nest. This could take several weeks, so patience is a must. If there is no indication that the male is interested, use your fallback pair.

Check out the size of that bubble nest.

Keep the female's separate tank at 78 degrees Fahrenheit. Have a small bit of Java Moss in it along with a rock cave. That way she's got a couple places to hide and will become comfortable in her tank... but at the same time you can lift her out with your net when you need to.

Another thing that will help stimulate the male to build a bubble nest is to float something small on top of the water. One attractive option is to put in a little bit of Crystalwort (Riccia Fluitans), a floating pond plant that produces beautiful green branches. If nothing else, you can always cut off the bottom of a Styrofoam cup and float that.

Other than that, your male's tank should be empty so he'll have an easier job gathering the eggs later on.

Introducing the Female

When vertical lines begin to appear on the female, and she has grown fatter (indicating her eggs are mature), she is ready to breed. Some females may also exhibit a bright white gravid tube protruding from behind the anal fin.

Introduce the female to the male's tank. Raise the temperature of the tank to 82 degrees. Once the temperature's raised, lower the water level to about 4 or 5 inches. This simulates the dry season of Southeast Asia, which is what triggers Bettas to start mating in the wild. At this point the male should start building a bubble nest if he hasn't already.

Watch for signs of extreme aggression. Chasing and some mild aggression is normal at first. Don't worry if a fin gets torn, but if the male attacks aggressively, remove the female back to the other tank and try again each day until the male either accepts her or it becomes obvious that he has no plans to. In that case, switch to your backup pair.

Spawning

When spawning occurs, the male coaxes the female to the bubble nest... at which point they proceed to dance. The male wraps himself around the female and extracts her eggs, releasing sperm at the same time. This will continue until all of the eggs have been extracted. At that point, the male will chase the female away from the nest. Remove the female when this occurs or the male will kill her.

The male will then gather the eggs and place them into the bubble nest, where he tends to them to prepare them for hatching.

Treat both tanks with a fungicide at this point to prevent fungus from forming on the fish or their eggs.

The male will stay busy keeping the eggs in the nest and he may refuse food until the fry hatch which normally occurs 24 to 36 hours after the spawning.

Caring for the Fry

Wait 24 hours before feeding the fry. At that time you can give them baby brine shrimp, daphnia, microworms, or commercially available liquid fry food. The fry will need to be fed 4 to 5 times a day.

Make sure the tank is covered with a tight lid, or if that's not available use plastic wrap from your kitchen. This allows the air above the water surface to have a high level of humidity, which helps each fry's labyrinth to develop. Failure to take this crucial step can cause most of the fry to drown.

Change the tank water every other day.

Remove the male from the tank once the fry are free-swimming.

When the fry have reached about one inch in length you can begin feeding them ground-up adult Betta food. Reduce the number of feedings to 2-3 a day.

When the fry reach about 4 weeks old, the males will begin chasing each other. That's the time to separate the more aggressive males into their own individual tanks or bowls.

The females can be kept together for 3-4 more weeks unless they start showing signs of aggression sooner.

Mouth Brooders

While most species of Betta are "bubble nesters" some species are "mouth brooders." This means that the male holds the eggs in his mouth until the fry hatch. This is not a common practice for the types of Betta that we normally see.

Don't Give Up

Don't be discouraged if your first breeding attempts fail. Your pair may simply not be "in the mood" or there may be environmental conditions at work. Even external conditions like sudden changes in atmospheric conditions can affect your Betta's mating urge.

Breeding Better Bettas

There are so many variables involved with Bettas – color, patterns, fins – that you need to make a plan for what you want to do. If you just breed willy-nilly, you'll end up with all sorts of weird (and sometimes undesirable) combinations that often have little or no market value or even any aesthetic appeal. And once, for example, a color gets mixed into a bloodline that you don't want – like green into a red betta – it could take decades to breed it out.

But it's all up to what YOU want. It could be that you're just looking to have nice pets rather than show-quality bettas that will impress your friends and bring you high prices if you decide to sell them. If you're serious about breeding, however, I recommend joining the International Betta Congress at http://www.ibcbettas.org and learning about the IBC's standards so that you know what you're aiming for before you start to breed your little ones..

Chapter 8: Bucks From Bettas?

Once you become successful at breeding Bettas, you may want to start selling Bettas yourself. There are many reasons why you may want to do this.

First is the simple numbers. If you do a great job raising your little ones, you could end up with literally hundreds of Bettas. That becomes too much for anyone to take care of!

With that in mind, you can make some money to defray your costs of Betta keeping (hey, what's "betta" than enjoying your Bettas on someone else's dime?). Even if you don't make a profit, whatever revenues you do get will at least make your hobby less expensive.

A final reason for going into breeding is to spread the strains that you create! Betta breeding is a very dynamic field. You may find yourself creating unique spawn with one-of-a-kind color and fin combinations.

I've done in-depth interviews with over two dozen professional breeders in the course of my research -- and I've gone into breeding myself. In this section I'm going to reveal the insider secrets that will get you well launched. (Please note that you can lose money and all advice is subject to the earnings disclaimer at the beginning of this book.)

Where to Sell Them

If you don't have your own site, probably the best place to sell Bettas on the internet are Aquabid.com (which is sort of the "eBay" of live fish selling). You can also sell through the "Betta Talk" section of the popular AroFanatics forum at http://www.arofanatics.com/forums

What I really recommend is getting your own website, however. I use

Namecheap.com for my domain name registrations and Dream Host for my site hosting, which you can get to by going to http://bettalovers.com/host

When you get your own site, you can sell Bettas the best by:

- Having a picture of each fish for sale, along with a sales page for each.

- Writing a long description of the fish. As a general rule, the more you say about the fish, the faster it will sell.

Some General Guidelines for Having a Betta Selling Business

Do not get involved in selling Bettas for the purpose of fighting. Not only is this cruel to the fish, but you will also be blacklisted and ostracized from the breeding community... which severely limits your ability to make sales. Besides, people these days buy Bettas based on things like their beautiful colors and fins, not fighting ability.

Join the International Betta Congress at http://www.ibcbettas.com It's absolutely a must. You'll get a treasure trove of excellent information, plus you'll have access to Betta shows where you can learn more about breeding plus meet ravenous buyers. As an added bonus, if someone in your local area contacts the IBC asking where they can buy Bettas, the IBC will direct the person to you.

Set up a way to accept credit cards. Get a Business Account (quick and easy to sign up for) through this link: http://www.bettalovers.com/processor and you can accept payments from buyers.

I'll get into more in-depth information below, in my section on moving into becoming a full-time business.

Shipping Bettas

In order to serve customers who are beyond your local area, you'll need to learn how to safely ship Bettas so they arrive alive and unharmed.

- Purchase professional shipping boxes that are large enough for the quantity of fish you will be shipping.

- Purchase Styrofoam "peanuts" or blocks that can be cut and hollowed as needed.

- Place each fish into its own plastic bag filled with approximately 2 inches more water than it takes to cover the fish. Do not fill the bag to the top as you are going to have to create an air bubble to keep the Betta from dying.

- Purchase a can of O_2 (canned oxygen) from your local pet supply store. Fill the bag with the oxygen and twist it closed immediately. Make sure that an air bubble exists. Seal the bag tightly with a twist tie.

- Place the plastic bag inside of another plastic bag and seal that one.

- Place the double sealed bag into a third bag and seal that one. This way your fish has a chance of surviving if the main bag bursts.

- Ship FedEx, UPS, or USPS OVERNIGHT. If you are shipping into or from a cold climate, add a heat pack to the container. Heat packs can be purchased from your local pet supply store.

- Spread a thick layer of peanuts on the bottom of the box, place the bag in the center, and fill the rest of the box with peanuts.

- If you are using a block, carve a hole in the block that's deep enough to cover ¾ of the bag when the bag is inserted. Do not cut completely through the bottom of the block. Cut the block to fit snugly inside of the box.

- Close and seal the box with professional shipping tape.

- Label the box clearly with your return address and the name, address, and telephone number of the recipient.

- Mark the box "Live Fish – Please Handle Carefully" somewhere near the shipping label.

- Insure the shipment for the value of the fish plus your shipping costs. That way if the box is lost or delayed, you will be reimbursed for your loss. You are not insuring the "life" of the fish, so if it dies from anything other than obvious abuse or neglect by the shipper, you may be out of luck.

Selling to Pet Stores

You'll find a massive amount of potential in your local area. Pet stores sell a lot of Bettas, and they're always looking for cheap suppliers.

Go into the store and ask to speak with the owner. Don't right off the bat tell them you have Bettas for sale, but instead start off with building a rapport with the store owner. Only then should you bring up that you have extra bettas you can supply to his or her store.

When talking price, don't make yourself sound over-eager. Instead if you get an offer of (for example) $2.50 a fish, say, "I need to run some numbers but I think that could work. I'll need to get back with you for certain."

Make sure of course that the store treats its Bettas well. Insist that the store keep the Bettas in tanks of at least 1 gallon each. Explain to the store manager thoroughly about why this is important and how it's inhumane to cram a Betta into a tiny cup.

Is a Betta Business Right for Me?

Just about every person has had the thought of starting their own business -- but most of them don't. There are a great many reasons why people don't take their ideals of running a business past thoughts alone. Perhaps they fear quitting the comforts of a regular paycheck. Some fear that they lack the aptitude or commitment to follow through with it.

It takes a lot of gumption for anyone to have the courage to start their own business. A retail business is one of the hardest businesses to run; the reason of course is the competition. There are literally millions of retail businesses operating across the world. Hundreds of thousands of these go under every year.

Running a business can be a frustrating thing to do at times, but it can also be very rewarding. There are a great many reasons why a person might want to start their own retail business, but before you do, you should ask yourself these questions first…

1.   Can I afford to open my own Betta business?

2.   Do I have the right attitude to start my own business?

3.   Can I handle the decision making process as a business owner?

4.   How good am I at multi-tasking?

5.   Can I handle the stress of being a business owner?

6.   Do I feel comfortable being someone else's boss?

7.   How are my abilities in dealing with people?

8.   Am I a self starter?

9.   How well can I get organized?

10.   Am I a driven enough person?

11.   How will starting my own business affect my family?

If you can honestly give a good answer to these questions, then you are a perfect candidate to own your own Betta business. These are some of the most important questions that you can ask yourself when considering opening up your own business.

Know Your Strengths

Here is a list of some of the things that you are going to have to know about if you want to run your own business:

- Basic bookkeeping: So that you can keep an accurate account of all of the money you pay, the money you get, and what is left afterwards. If you don't know your numbers, you will fail. Get a program like Quickbooks and learn how to use it.

- How much money is needed to get started. Ideally of course it won't be much at all, as you've already put in the money you needed when you got the aquariums, equipment and so forth.

- Stock and inventory: You have to be able to keep track of the Bettas you intend to sell.

- Payroll: You have to be able to keep enough money to pay yourself and any employees and keep track of monies paid.

- Marketing: You will need to know how to market your Bettas in an appealing way, keep up with demand, and monitor the buying trends of your customers.

- Basic economics: You will need to be able to follow consumer and Betta show trends so you can breed the right strains and maintain a profit for your business.

- Networking: It is necessary for you to gather and maintain business contacts. They will prove invaluable to you at times.

- Legalities: Be sure to protect yourself by forming an appropriate company structure – S-corp, C-corp, sole proprietorship, LLC, etc. You'll also need to get whatever business licenses are required by your government. Check with a business attorney in your area to find out what's best for you.

- What management controls are needed. You might, for example, hire someone who's highly sales oriented to talk to pet store owners for you, paying them a commission if they can net you a sale.

These are just some of the things that you are going to have to know in order to maintain a good business. If you find that you will have problems doing some of these things, then you should get someone else to handle them for you. Better that than lose money in the end.

Know Your Competition

In many cases, you'll find that the best way to compete with your competition is to not compete at all, especially if they have established a long and trusted reputation with their consumers. You do not want to alienate your competition or build feuds with them because they can be a source of great help to you if you know how to approach them.

Here are some good examples of ways that you can create a good rapport with them:

1. Offer to be an affiliate of theirs. This way you can ensure that they will send business your way if they can't meet the needs of a customer that you can supply.

2. Don't try to market your prices as a better bargain. Studies have shown that the least profitable way to compete is on price. Instead focus on service and quality.

3. Assess your competitor's success rate. Learn what they are doing that is so great and offer something better.

You should also keep your eye on their marketing and promotional techniques because it will help you to keep up with them better.

Marketing

This is something you will already have an idea about when you put together your business plan. Nothing is better for an emerging business than a really good marketing strategy. This is when all of your research will work to your advantage. In order to build a good marketing strategy you must first:

- Correctly assess your competition and what they are doing to market their businesses. You have to offer your consumers something that is fresh and different if you want to get their attention.

- Study your potential market so you can establish what your consumers are missing in their current needs. Find out what they want and give it to them.

- Learn what types of sales pitches work best with pet stores, online hobbyists, and other potential customers.

- The key to successful marketing is meeting the basic supply and demand of your target market. Be sure to stay on top of this because these things are always changing.

- You should be able to keep up with market changes and try to anticipate them beforehand because it keeps you in tune with the average consumer. This will prove invaluable to you later.

Credit Problems

The worst thing an entrepreneur can do is to run the business on too much credit. It just goes without saying that you have to run your business within your means. All too often business owners find themselves buying things the business simply doesn't need. This is a big no-no in the business world.

Once a business spends too much money on credit, they learn all too late that the interest rates on credit cards can force hundreds of extra dollars in expenses. New businesses just can't afford to pay them. There is also the fact that over-buying supplies and merchandise can be a far bigger problem than businesses expect.

Any successful business owner knows that you start off small and build your way up. Don't run your business above your means.

Taxes

The unseasoned entrepreneur can easily fall prey to the government. Poor calculation can be a costly problem, but failing to properly fill out your tax forms, and missing valuable monies can be a problem as well. Sometimes it is simply an issue of filing your taxes late. Keeping up with your fiscal year's end can be frightfully easy to forget.

A good accountant will help you avoid common tax problems like these and others.

Breeding Business Summary

By now, you should know the nuts and bolts of selling Bettas, and you should know if starting a Betta breeder business of your own is right for you. If you have, you should learn all the things you will need to be aware of in order to get it up and running. Hopefully you have also realized that running your own Betta business takes a lot more than mere desire.

Don't expect to ever make a profit selling Bettas. Especially at first, the main reason to sell them is to subsidize your hobby, and that's it.

Finally, at all times remember to run an ethical business. Insist that pet stores you do business with give the Bettas a comfortable living environment. Do not sell to individuals who will mistreat the Bettas. The bottom line is that the welfare of your little ones is more important than money.

Whether you go into breeding for fun or profit, I wish you the best of luck!

Always make sure the little ones you sell will be as well-treated as Rho, the guy in this picture. (Source: Mendel, Wikimedia)

Chapter 9: Dealing With Grief and Loss of Your Betta

It doesn't matter if it's a fish or a human; grief and sadness are natural emotions that everyone feels when they suffer the loss of a loved one.

Grief over the loss of your pet Betta is normal. The expression of our grief is a natural way to start the emotional healing we must do to restore balance to our lives.

It's possible that friends and family members will not understand why you are grieving. After all, it was "just a fish" they say. They might not realize that you derived a lot of pleasure from your Betta, and that you are going to miss the way he wiggled his tail when he saw you and the clever things he did in his tank. You two had bonded. You became best friends.

Range of Emotions

Your grief over the loss of your Betta can manifest itself in many ways including:

- Guilt if you feel responsible for his death in some way.

- Denial, which may make it difficult for you to accept that your pet has actually died.

- Anger at yourself or the person or circumstances that caused your fish's death.

- Depression which can cause you to cry, skip work, sleep excessively, or experience physical symptoms such as upset stomach, vomiting and headaches.

How to Handle Your Feelings

- Start out by accepting your feelings. Don't try to bury or deny them. The grief process will play itself out and you will eventually start feeling better. How long it takes depends a lot on how willing you are to be open and honest about your feelings.

- Find a friend, family member or other pet lover you can talk to. Pick someone who will be sympathetic and won't try to belittle your feelings.

- If you can't find someone to talk to on your own, ask your vet or the local humane society for some recommendations. These people deal with pet loss regularly and they have a lot of contacts.

Decide How to Handle the Remains

You can bury your pet on your property, but understand that you run the risk of having it dug up by a wild animal that picks up the scent.

If your fish had died in the wild then it would have eventually sunk to the bottom and become part of the ecosystem. Perhaps letting your fish go into a large body of water would be a good option.

How to Tell the Children

Death is a natural process. Your children need to understand that nothing lives forever. Be patient and gentle when you tell them. Don't lie and tell them that you gave the fish away or that it "escaped" and disappeared. Tell them that the fish died. Don't blame the cat, even if the cat was the culprit. If "fishy heaven" is an appropriate concept in your home, then the fish went there.

Remember that your children will be grieving as well. Have a good cry together. It has medicinal value.

How Soon Should I Wait Before Getting a New Betta?

That's entirely up to you. If you can deal with a new fish in your life immediately, then that's as good a time as any. Just make sure you are emotionally capable of handling having a new Betta in your old Betta's tank.

But What If I'm Having a *Really* Tough Time Getting Over My Grief?

Let's be perfectly clear. Loss of a Betta can be tough. You spent so long keeping the fish alive and happy, and bonded with them, and then they die.

The first thing to realize is that intense bereavement for a pet is totally normal. In fact, psychologists have said that in many cases, grief for a close pet can be just as strong as it is for a close relative. Don't listen to your friends who tell you things like "just get over it" and "it was just a fish."

If you're having a brutally tough time getting over the sorrow of losing your Betta, there's a step-by-step recovery guide I highly recommend. It's called ***How to ROAR: Pet Loss Grief Recovery*** by Robin Jean Brown. You can find it by going to http://www.petlossguide.com

Chapter 10: Training Bettas

Bettas are very friendly fish, despite their sometimes-aggressive behavior towards others of their species, and they respond well to training. Like most animals, Bettas respond well to food as a training aid and reward. This is known as "operant conditioning."

Basically, that means your Betta will respond to a certain stimulus (in our case, a "magic stick" that you wave like a wand) if he psychologically associates that stimulus with a certain reward (in our case, food!).

Here are some training best practices:

- Purchase a feeding stick that you can attach food to. It's like a small "magic wand" with a curved or hooked end for holding the food.

- Introduce the Betta to the stick by using it during normal feeding. The goal is to get him to recognize that the presence of the stick means it's time to eat.

- Your first "trick" will be training the Betta to eat the food from the stick.

- Hold the food end of the stick slightly below the water surface level. If your Betta does not immediately come to investigate, wave it under the water gently to spread the food odor and to attract his attention. Hold the stick still once your Betta responds, to avoid scaring it. Do not move or jerk the stick while he is retrieving the food.

- Repeat this process every day until the Betta automatically responds to the presence of the stick.

Congratulations! You've taught him his first simple trick. Build upon the stick relationship by teaching your fish to spin around.

- Present the stick and food as normal. As the fish approaches the stick, move it slowly in a small circle so he follows it. This may not happen at first, but with patience, it will happen within a few days of trying.

With some practice and patience, you can use the feeding stick to teach your Betta to swim through hoops, chase his tail, roll over, and nearly anything else you want, merely by moving the stick and having your fish follow it.

Another really neat trick is to teach your Betta how to jump out of the water and grab the food from your "magic stick":

- All you need to do is feed your Betta from the stick closer and closer to the surface each time. Eventually you feed him right at the surface of the water. Once he's used to that, you can raise the stick slightly above the water and your Betta will jump for it!

Follow the stick (from outside the tank!):

- This trick will dazzle your friends. Once your Betta has been conditioned to follow the "magic stick of happiness," you can simply put it next to the glass wall and your little guy will swim right up to it! At that point, all you need to do is move it on the outside of the glass, in whatever pattern you want... and your fish will move at your very command.

Jump through a hoop!:

- Locate a small plastic ring that your Betta can fit through. That will be your hoop.

- Place the hoop in the aquarium, leaving it there for about a week or so, so that your Betta will become used to it.

- At first your Betta will be reluctant to swim through the loop to get at the "magic stick." Just keep working with him, and eventually when he goes through the loop give him a reward with the feeding stick.

By the way, you can also use your finger instead of the "magic stick" if you wish. Just have the food on your finger instead of the feeding stick on all of the instructions above.

Betta Fitness

Bettas need exercise! Otherwise, in the luxury of your house, they can grow spoiled, lazy, and out of shape. Similar to the way hamsters run in wheels, you can create a "Betta Wheel" for your little one to swim through.

All you need to do is this... Get a straw and put it in the water. Start stirring around and around, until there's a gentle circulation of water, swirling around the tank. This will induce your Betta to swim, giving him a bit of physical fitness.

Chapter 11: Betta Information on the Internet

The Internet is rife with websites that cater especially to the Betta fish. Here are some of my favorites:

- International Betta Congress - http://www.ibcbettas.org

  As previously mentioned, this is a must-join, especially if you're going to become involved with breeding. The International Betta Congress (IBC) is an organization dedicated to the keeping, breeding, showing, and protection of Betta Splendens and wild type Bettas.

- AquaBid.com

  You can buy and sell aquarium equipment and higher-quality Betta fish on AquaBid.com. Use their search feature and type the word "Betta" to see all of their Betta-related auctions. Word of warning about the site itself -- be sure to have a pop-up blocker installed before visiting, otherwise AquaBid will flood you with pop-up windows.

- BettaDreams.com

  A good source of information on Betta Splendens, Siamese fighting fish, information and stock.

- Betta Benevolence - http://groups.msn.com/BettaBenevolance (Note the incorrect spelling.)

  A lively and spirited discussion forum focused on Betta Splendens. There you'll find many members who will help you with your questions.

- Betta Splendens - http://groups.msn.com/BettaSplendens

A large discussion group dedicated to raising, breeding and enjoying Betta Splendens.

- Betta Splendens Club - http://groups.msn.com/BettaSplendensClub

A small group of dedicated Betta owners who always welcome new members.

- The Fish That Threatened National Security - http://www.post-gazette.com/pg/03362/255283.stm

A very cute story about a Betta Fish and the failure of the Department of Homeland Security to bring about its execution by "flushing."

That's all for now

I hope that you enjoyed reading this book as much as I enjoyed writing it. Bettas are incredible little fish. They show you when they're happy and they show you when they're not. They're bright, easy to care for, relatively inexpensive, and come in a wide variety of colors. They're also crafty, imaginative, noble, pompous, brainy, and have their own way of doing things that makes them happy. And all of this is for our enjoyment. You can admire their entertaining antics for hours. It doesn't get any better than that. Enjoy!